GROW YOUR OWN
GREEN BEANS

BY LISA J. AMSTUTZ

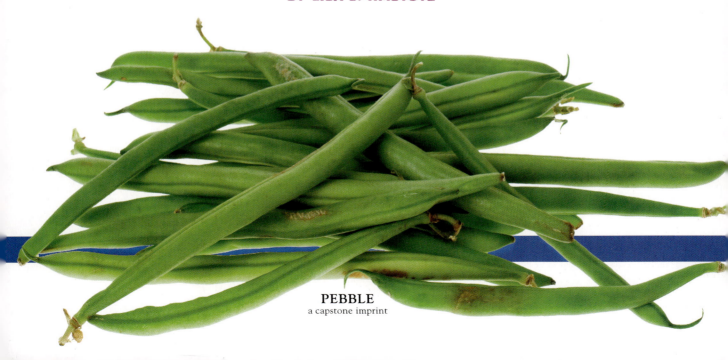

PEBBLE
a capstone imprint

Published by Pebble, an imprint of Capstone
1710 Roe Crest Drive, North Mankato, Minnesota 56003
capstonepub.com

Copyright © 2025 by Capstone. All rights reserved. No part of this publication may be reproduced in whole or in part, or stored in a retrieval system, or transmitted in any form or by any means, electronic, mechanical, photocopying, recording, or otherwise, without written permission of the publisher.

Library of Congress Cataloging-in-Publication Data is available on the Library of Congress website.
ISBN: 9780756589509 (hardcover)
ISBN: 9780756589714 (paperback)
ISBN: 9780756589547 (ebook PDF)

Summary: How to plant and care for a green bean plant is described in simple steps accompanied by clear photos. How to harvest the green beans and the science behind plant growth are also covered.

Editorial Credits
Editor: Erika L. Shores; Designer: Heidi Thompson; Media Researcher: Jo Miller; Production Specialist: Tori Abraham

Image Credits
Getty Images: brytta, 17, ognianm, 20, Yellow Dog Productions, 19; Shutterstock: amenic181, cover (middle), amenic181, 10, Andrii Bezvershenko, 23 (bottom), Aseprudi72, 13, Digihelion, 21, Eric Gevaert, back cover, 1, 16, greenair, cover (right), Hunter Leader, 23 (top right), Levent Konuk, 6 (left), Liz Weber, 15, Mallinka1, 23 (top left), NonTheerachai, 6 (right), Pawel_Brzozowski, cover (top) 7 (bottom), Peter Hermes Furian, 18, PickOne, 9, Pixel-Shot, 7 (top), Singkham, cover (bottom left), 12, Vadym Sh, 5, Yekatseryna Netuk, 11

The publisher and the author shall not be liable for any damages allegedly arising from the information in this book, and they specifically disclaim any liability from the use or application of any of the contents of this book.

Any additional websites and resources referenced in this book are not maintained, authorized, or sponsored by Capstone. All product and company names are trademarks™ or registered® trademarks of their respective holders.

Printed and bound in China. 5097

TABLE OF CONTENTS

Cool Beans 4

What You Need 6

What You Do 8

Take It Further 20

Behind the Science 22

Glossary 24

About the Author 24

Words in **BOLD** are in the glossary.

COOL BEANS

Do you like to eat green beans? You can grow your own! All you need is a sunny spot outdoors.

No space? That's okay. Try growing beans in a pot. Set it outside in a sunny place.

WHAT YOU NEED

- green bean seeds
- **rake**
- water
- watering can
- a sunny garden spot

WHAT YOU DO

STEP 1

Wait until the **frost date** has passed. You can look it up online. Then it is safe to plant beans.

Pick a spot in your garden that gets 6 to 8 hours of sun each day. Get the soil ready. Clear away grass and weeds. Smooth the soil with the rake.

STEP 2

Push seeds into the soil. They should be 1 inch (2.5 centimeters) deep. Plant them 2 inches (5 cm) apart. Want more than one row? Space them 18 inches (45.7 cm) apart.

Cover the seeds with soil. Pat the soil down gently. Then water the seeds. The soil should be damp.

STEP 3

Soon the seeds will **sprout**. It takes a week or two. The plants grow fast.

Look out for pests! Pick off bugs. Bean leaf beetles can harm beans. Pull weeds near your plants too.

STEP 4

Watch your plants grow tall. This takes a month or two. Water them each week if the soil is dry.

The plants will **bloom**. Each flower makes a tiny bean. It grows bigger each day.

STEP 5

Wait until the beans are 4 inches (10 cm) long. Then it is time to **harvest** them. The beans should be firm but not bumpy. Pinch them off at the **stem**.

Check your plants each day. Pick the ripe beans. Then more will grow.

STEP 6

Wash your beans well. Snap off the stems. Now they are ready to cook. Ask an adult to help you steam or boil them. Add a little salt and butter. Enjoy!

TAKE IT FURTHER

It is easy to save bean seeds. Leave a few beans on the plant. Wait until they get dry and brown. Then harvest the seeds. Keep them in a cool, dry place. You can plant them next year!

BEHIND THE SCIENCE

Plants can't grow in the dark. They need light! They need air, water, and **nutrients** too. Plants use these to make sugars. This food helps them grow.

GLOSSARY

bloom (BLOOM)—to flower

frost date (FROST DAYT)—the date when the last frost comes in an area

harvest (HAR-vist)—to gather crops that are ripe

nutrients (NOO-tree-uhnts)—parts of food, like vitamins, that are used for growth

rake (RAYK)—a garden tool with metal or wood teeth

sprout (SPROUT)—to start to grow

stem (STEM)—the part of a plant that connects the roots to the leaves and flowers

ABOUT THE AUTHOR

Lisa J. Amstutz is the author of more than 150 children's books on topics ranging from applesauce to zebra mussels. An ecologist by training, she enjoys sharing her love of nature with kids. Lisa lives on a small farm with her family.